Let's Investigate Plants!



# How Plants Defend Themselves

By Ruth Owen

KidHaven PUBLISHING

Published in 2024 by
**KidHaven Publishing, an Imprint of Greenhaven Publishing, LLC**
2544 Clinton St., Buffalo, NY 14224



Portions of this work were originally authored by Ruth Owen and published as *How Do Plants Defend Themselves?*
All new material this edition authored by Ruth Owen.

Produced for Rosen by Ruby Tuesday Books Ltd
Editor for Ruby Tuesday Books Ltd: Mark J. Sachner
US Editor: Designer: Emma Randall

Photo Credits:
Cover, 1, 4–5, 6–7, 8–9, 12–13, 14–15, 18, 20–21, 22–23, 24, 25 (top),
26–27, 28–29 © Shutterstock; 10–11, 19 (bottom), 25 (bottom) © FLPA;
16–17, 19 (top) © Wikipedia Creative Commons.

Cataloging-in-Publication Data

Names: Owen, Ruth.
Title: How plants defend themselves / Ruth Owen.
Description: Buffalo, New York : KidHaven Publishing, 2024. | Series: Let's investigate plants! | Includes glossary and index.
Identifiers: ISBN 9781534545601 (pbk.) | ISBN 9781534545618 (library bound) | ISBN 9781534545625 (ebook)
Subjects: LCSH: Plant defenses--Juvenile literature. | Plants, Protection of--Juvenile literature.
Classification: LCC QK921.O94 2024 | DDC 581.4'7--dc23



Manufactured in the United States of America

CPSIA compliance information: Batch #CSKH24: For further information contact Greenhaven Publishing LLC at 1-844-317-7404.

Please visit our website, www.greenhavenpublishing.com.
For a free color catalog of all our high-quality books, call toll free 1-844-317-7404 or fax 1-844-317-7405.

Find us on

# Contents


Don't Eat Me! .......... 4
Prickly Protection .......... 6
Storing Water in Barrels .......... 8
When Spines Don't Work! .......... 10
Keeping Cool .......... 12
Thorny Trunks and Branches .......... 14
Whistling Thorn Trees .......... 16
Prickly Defenses .......... 18
Pretty but Poisonous .......... 20
Deadly Wolfsbane .......... 22
Berries That Can Kill! .......... 24
Ouch! Stinging Nettles .......... 26
Let's Investigate Cacti .......... 28
Glossary .......... 30
Websites .......... 31
Read More, Index, Answers .......... 32

# Don't Eat Me!

**Plants can make their own food. They can reproduce by growing flowers, fruits, and seeds. However, there's something they cannot do—run! If a hungry animal wants to eat a plant, how does a plant defend itself?**

To avoid becoming animal food, some **species** of plants have developed the **adaptation** of protective **spines**. Others have a defensive covering of vicious **thorns** on their stems.

These beautiful angel's trumpets flowers are very poisonous.

Some plant species, however, have a means of defense that cannot be seen. These plants produce powerful **toxins** in their roots, stems, leaves, and flowers. The poisonous substances usually make the plant taste or smell bad. They can do serious harm to any creature that dares to take a bite!

# Prickly Protection

**The plant world's masters of prickly protection are cacti. These spiky plants grow spines to keep animals from eating them.**

Cacti grow in hot, dry **habitats**, such as **deserts**. Very little rain falls in deserts, so cacti have adapted to this lack of regular rain by storing water. When rain eventually does fall, cacti store as much water as possible in their thick, fleshy stems.

The only problem with this survival adaptation, however, is that it makes a cactus very attractive to desert animals. By eating a cactus's stems, an animal can obtain both food and water. Therefore, in order to defend against hungry, thirsty animals, cacti have sharp, protective spines.

A prickly pear's fleshy, spine-covered pads look like leaves but are actually the plant's stems.

A saguaro cactus's main stem and arms can store enormous quantities of water.

# Storing Water in Barrels

**A barrel cactus's stems have ribs that expand and contract, like an accordion. When it rains, the plant takes in as much water as possible from the ground through its roots. Its ribs expand to allow the plant's sponge-like flesh to soak up gallons of water.**

The fat, round stems of the cacti act like water barrels and give this plant its name.

Once **hydrated**, the swollen stems of a barrel cactus may be over 90 percent water. In fact, during very dry times, a large plant can survive for more than five years by using its stored water.

With its juicy, water-soaked flesh, a barrel cactus is very **vulnerable** to thirsty desert animals, so the plant grows a dense covering of sharp, protective spines.

barrel cacti growing in a desert

# When Spines Don't Work!

**You might think that cacti are perfectly safe from hungry and thirsty animals, but some creatures are determined to get a meal of spiny cactus.**

Land iguanas are large lizards that live on the Galápagos Islands. In their hot, dry habitat, fresh water is scarce, so land iguanas feed on prickly pear cacti both as food and as a way to obtain water. Before eating, the lizards sometimes scrape large spines from the plants with their front feet. With their tough, leathery mouths, however, they are adapted to just munch into the cacti and eat the spines!

Some animals, such as rats, are small enough to move around between a cactus's spines. For these desert animals, cacti are an important source of food and water.

Galápagos land iguana

# Keeping Cool

**A cactus's spines deter its hungry neighbors from feeding on its juicy flesh, but that's not all. The plant's spines can also help keep the cactus cool. How?**

Deserts are usually wide-open places. There are no large, leafy trees to create shade. Temperatures during the day in summer may reach 140° Fahrenheit (60°C). Like any living thing, a plant can be damaged by the scorching heat of the sun. Cacti, however, have their own personal sunscreens.

Teddy bear cholla cacti get their name from their densely packed spines that look like fuzzy fur.

A cactus spine might only be as thick as a needle, but it makes a thin, cooling shadow on the plant's stem. When there are thousands of spines, and each spine makes a shadow, it's enough to help shade a cactus from the desert sun.

# Thorny Trunks and Branches

**Like cacti, some species of trees protect their stems. These plants grow dagger-like thorns on their trunks and branches.**

Silk floss trees are truly beautiful plants that produce a mass of pink flowers in spring. Take a close-up look at the tree's trunk, though, and you'll see that it's covered with thousands of spiky thorns.

silk floss tree

thorns on a silk floss tree's trunk

Thorny acacia trees grow on dry **grasslands** in Africa. With few plants around and lots of hungry plant eaters, these trees grow sharp thorns to protect their leaves from being eaten. Not every animal is put off by the trees' weaponry, however. Giraffes are able to twist and turn their 20-inch (50 cm) tongues between the thorns to grab the leaves.

# Whistling Thorn Trees

**Some kinds of acacia trees have protective thorns and a second means of defense—thousands of stinging ants!**

The thorns of whistling acacia trees have round, swollen bases. Ants make their homes in the bases of the thorns and feed on a sweet liquid called **sap** that's produced by the tree's leaves. If another animal tries to eat the tree's leaves, the ants sting the intruder's mouth. The ants are protecting their food source, but at the same time, they help protect the tree from being eaten.

Whistling thorn trees get their name because they make a whistling noise. The rounded bases of the thorns, where the ants live, have tiny entrance and exit holes. The whistling sound is made when wind blows over these holes.

ants

# Prickly Defenses

**The life of a roadside blackberry bush or a rose plant blooming in a garden might not seem that exciting. However, day and night, these plants are in a battle for survival.**

Rose plants grow colorful, scented flowers that attract bees and other insects that **pollinate** the flowers so the plant can produce seeds. Blackberry bushes produce leaves, flowers, and seeds inside sweet berries. These plant parts taste good to many animals. As a means of defense, the stems of these plants produce thorns. Some thorns are large, hard, and woody. Other thorns grow as a mass of tiny, hairlike prickles.

A prickly defense doesn't always stop animals from eating a plant, however. Goats, deer, and many other plant-eaters will do battle with painful thorns to feed on new green **shoots**, tasty roses, or juicy blackberries.

Even the thinnest stems of this blackberry bush are smothered in tiny prickles.

This beautiful rose plant has stems covered in savage thorns!

# Pretty but Poisonous

**Some plants don't have spines or thorns, but hungry animals still avoid them. That's because the plant's roots, stems, leaves, flowers, or fruits contain deadly toxins.**

Scientists don't know for sure how animals learn to avoid eating poisonous plants. The poisons may make the plants taste unpleasant.

These yellow flowers are poisonous buttercups.

Sometimes animals might eat a small amount of a plant, get sick, and then learn not to eat that plant again. Young animals watch their mothers and learn which plants the adults avoid eating. The knowledge of which plants are dangerous is then passed on from generation to generation.

Buttercups and foxgloves are two poisonous wild plants that often grow thickly in pastures where sheep, horses, and other grazing animals live. The animals will avoid these plants, however, eating every other plant around them.

# Deadly Wolfsbane

**Monkshood, or aconitum, plants grow pretty blue and purple flowers. They can be found in gardens and in wild places.**

These deadly plants are sometimes called wolfsbane. This name comes from ancient times when the plants were used to kill wolves that attacked sheep. Shepherds are said to have poisoned wolves by placing wolfsbane inside pieces of meat.

Aconitum is also known as monkshood because its flowers are shaped like the hood of a monk's cloak.

Every part of these pretty plants is poisonous. Eating just a tiny piece of an aconitum causes severe stomach pains and vomiting. The plant's poison also makes the heart slow down and even stop beating! People have even been poisoned by touching the plant and absorbing its poisons through their skin or through a wound.

# Berries That Can Kill!

**Many plants grow berries as protective coverings for their seeds. To stop animals from eating the berries and destroying the seeds, some plants have highly poisonous berries.**

The berries of deadly nightshade and pokeweed plants can kill an animal or person. In fact, deadly nightshade berries are among the most dangerous berries in the world.

Sometimes, however, berries that can kill most other animals don't harm birds. This is because plants need birds to spread their seeds to new growing places. A bird eats a berry, then the seeds pass unharmed through the animal's **digestive system**. Later, the seeds leave the bird's body in its waste and land on the ground, ready to start growing.

deadly nightshade berries

These pokeweed berries look delicious but are very toxic.

# Ouch! Stinging Nettles

**They grow at roadsides, on wasteland, and in wild places and don't much look as if they could hurt us—but ouch! Touch a stinging nettle and you'll feel its powerful defenses.**

Just the lightest brush against the leaves or stems of a stinging nettle, and hundreds of tiny hairs will inject a liquid into your skin that stings—a lot! Not all species of nettles are dangerous, but you should always be wary and careful around these plants.

Plants may not be able to run from people and other animals, but many plants are not defenseless. From stinging hairs to sharp spines, pointed thorns to powerful poisons, plants have developed very effective adaptations to defend themselves from becoming food for hungry animals.

# Let's Investigate Cacti

**How do spines keep a cactus cool?**

In this first investigation, make a model of a cactus that will show how the plant's spines create tiny, cooling shadows on its stems.

**YOU WILL NEED:**

- a small kitchen sponge
- a craft knife
- a small dish
- toothpicks

**Step 1:**
Use the craft knife to cut the sponge into the shape of a cactus. Stand the sponge cactus in the dish so it doesn't fall over.
*(Only use a knife if an adult is there to help you.)*

**Step 2:**
Push toothpicks into the sponge to create spines.

**Step 3:**
Place the sponge cactus in a sunny spot. Are the spines creating shadows?

**Why? How? What?**

How could your cactus receive more protection from the sun?
*(See page 32 for the answer.)*

## How do cacti store water?

In this second investigation, make a cactus model that can be used to show how these plants absorb and store water in their stems. You will also investigate how a cactus's waxy skin stops the water inside the plant's stems from drying out, or evaporating.

**YOU WILL NEED:**

- **two small kitchen sponges**
- **a craft knife**
- **two small dishes**
- **a measuring cup and water**
- **waxed paper**

**Step 1:**

Use the craft knife to cut each sponge into the shape of a cactus. You can reuse your cactus from investigation 1. Make sure both sponge cacti are the same shape and size. *(Only use a knife if an adult is there to help you.)*

**Step 2:**

Stand each cactus in a dish and pour a cup of water into each dish. Wait for the cacti to soak up the water—just like the flesh of a cactus absorbing water.

**Step 3:**

Remove the cacti from their dishes. Now wrap one of the sponge cacti in waxed paper. Leave the two cacti on a countertop to dry out.

**Why? How? What?**

Which sponge cactus dried out first?

Why do you think the cacti dried at different speeds?

*(See page 32 for the answer.)*

# Glossary

**adaptation** (a-dap-TAY-shun) A physical change or change in behavior that happens over time and makes a plant or animal more able to survive in its environment.

**deserts** (DEH-zurts) Places that receive less than 10 inches (25 cm) of rain or snow each year. Deserts can be hot or cold. They are often sandy or rocky, with few trees and other plants.

**digestive system** (dy-JES-tiv SIS-tem) The group of body parts, including the stomach and intestines, that break down food so that a body can use it for fuel.

**grasslands** (GRAS-landz) Hot habitats with lots of grass and few trees or bushes. Sometimes it is very dry, and at other times there is a lot of rain.

**habitats** (HA-buh-tats) Places where animals or plants normally live. A habitat may be a backyard, a forest, the ocean, or a mountainside.

**hydrated** (HY-dray-ted) Having absorbed water.

**pollinate** (PAH-luh-nayt) To move pollen from the anthers of one flower to the stigma of another.

**reproduce** (ree-pruh-DOOS) To make more of something, such as when plants make seeds that will grow into new plants.

**sap** (SAP) A liquid in the stems of plants that carries food and water throughout the plant.

**shoots** (SHOOTS) New parts of a plant, such as leaves, that emerge from underground or from a plant's stems.

**species** (SPEE-sheez) One type of living thing. The members of a species look alike and can reproduce together.

**spines** (SPYNZ) Thin, spiky parts that grow on the stems of cacti and protect the plants from being eaten by animals.

**thorns** (THORNZ) Pointed, hard parts of a plant's stem that protect the plant from being eaten by animals.

**toxins** (TOK-sinz) Harmful, poisonous substances.

**vulnerable** (VUL-nuh-ruh-bul) Able to be harmed.

# Websites

**https://www.desertusa.com/cactus/the-cactus.html**

**https://www.ducksters.com/science/biology/plant_defenses.php**

**https://www.britannica.com/list/7-of-the-worlds-deadliest-plants**

# Read More

**Hirsch, Rebecca E.** *When Plants Attack (Strange and Terrifying Plants).* Minneapolis, MN: Lerner Publishing Group, 2019.

**Hofer, Charles C.** *Silent But Deadly Plants (Killer Nature).* North Mankato, MN: Capstone Press, 2022.

**Loukopoulos, Beatrice.** *Plants with Thorns, Spines, and Prickles (Peculiar Plants of the World).* New York, NY: Rosen Publishing, 2019.

# Index

**A**
aconitums, 22–23
adaptations, 4, 6, 10, 27
ants, 16–17

**B**
bees, 18
berries, 24–25

**C**
cacti, 6–7, 8–9, 10–11, 12–13, 14, 28–29

**D**
deserts, 6, 8–9, 10, 12

**F**
foxgloves, 21

**G**
Galápagos land iguanas, 10–11
giraffes, 14–15

**L**
leaves, 5, 6, 14, 16, 18, 20, 26

**P**
poisons, 5, 20–21, 22–23, 24–25, 27
pollination, 18

**R**
roses, 4, 18–19

**S**
seeds, 18, 24
shadows, 12–13
spines, 4, 6–7, 8–9, 10, 12–13, 27
stems, 4–5, 6–7, 8, 12, 18–19, 20, 26
stinging nettles, 26

**T**
taste (of plants), 5, 18, 20
thorns, 4, 14–15, 16–17, 18–19, 27
toxins, 5, 20–21, 22–23, 24–25, 27
trees, 12, 14–15, 16–17

**W**
water, 6–7, 8, 10

# Answers

**Page 28**
One way for your sponge cactus to receive more protection is to add more spines. You can also try turning your cactus and watching how the shadows made by the spines change size and shape. Try to find a position for your cactus where as much of its stem as possible is covered with shade.

**Page 29**
The cactus sponge wrapped in waxed paper probably took longer to dry out. That's because the water inside that sponge did not evaporate as quickly as in the other sponge The sponge's waxy protective covering helped retain water, just as a cactus's waxy skin helps it retain its stored water.